Let's Party!

Written by
Rob Waring and **Maurice Jamall**
(with contributions by **Julian Thomlinson**)

Before You Read

to clean		guitar	
to dance		kitchen	
to pay		music	
to sing		parents	
accident		party	
chair		vase	
food		broken	

In the story

Jenny   Daniela   Alex   Gemma   Dad   Mom

"You can come, can't you?" Jenny asked. "Please?"
Jenny was talking to her friend, Daniela. "My parents are going away on Saturday, and I don't want to be in the house alone. So would you please come and stay over at my house that night?"

"I'd love to," replied Daniela. "That would be great. How about Alex? He's coming, isn't he?"

"Yes, I asked him today. He's not staying at my house, but he's bringing a movie," she said. "We can watch it together." Daniela replied, "That's a wonderful idea."

A school friend of Jenny's was listening. Her name was Gemma. "What's happening on Saturday?" she asked. Daniela said, "Alex and I are going to Jenny's house."

"Really?" said Gemma. "Is it a party?"

"No, we're going to watch a movie together. Her parents are away for the weekend," said Daniela.

"Oh, can I come?" asked Gemma.

"Well . . . ," said Jenny. "That will be difficult. It's not a party. I can't have many people there. You understand, don't you, Gemma?"

"Oh," said Gemma. "I see. That's okay."

Later, Daniela said to Jenny, "Jenny, why don't you have a party? It'll be fun. You can invite your friends."

"Umm," said Jenny. "I'd love to have a party, but my parents will say no. I'm sorry."

Daniela replied, "Then don't tell them. They'll be away all weekend and we'll have a lot of time to clean the house after the party."

"Well, I don't know," said Jenny. "I'll think about it."

"But we'll have a great time, Jenny, won't we?" asked Daniela. "You can invite just a few friends. It won't be a big party."

Jenny was thinking, "Daniela really wants a party. So it may be okay. Maybe it'll be fun."

She decided. "Okay," she agreed. "Let's have a party. But I don't want many people, okay? Just Faye, John, David, Tyler, you, Alex, and me. Ask them, will you?"

"That's very kind of you," said Daniela. "I can invite Yoon-Hee, can't I?" she asked. Yoon-Hee was one of Daniela's best friends. Jenny liked Yoon-Hee. She thought, "I think it'll be okay."

"Okay," agreed Jenny. "She can come. Please ask her, too."

"Thanks. What time do we come?" asked Daniela.

"My parents leave at about five o'clock in the afternoon. So how about coming around then?" asked Jenny.

"That's a good plan," replied Daniela. "We'll see you then."

It was Saturday, and Jenny was saying goodbye to her parents and sister, Jessica. They were getting in the car.
"What are you going to do when we're away?" her mother asked. "Are you going to study?"
"No, Mom. I'm going to watch a movie with Alex and Daniela," said Jenny. "After Alex goes home, Daniela and I will go to bed early."
Her mother replied, "Okay. Have a good time. But remember to do your homework, please."
"Okay, I will. Thanks, Mom," said Jenny.

Alex and Daniela arrived. "Hello," they said.
"Thank you, Mrs. Martin," said Daniela.
"You're welcome," she replied.
Alex said, "I have the movie. It's *Love on the Seas*."
Jenny's mother said, "Jenny, if you have any trouble,
please call Mrs. Smith, okay?"
"Oh, okay," said Jenny. "I will. Bye, Mom. Don't worry.
Everything will be okay."

Jenny's parents left. "Come in," Jenny said to Alex and Daniela. "Everything's ready."

"We brought some food and drinks," said Daniela.

"Oh, thanks," said Jenny. "When are the others coming?"

"Tyler, John, Faye, and David are coming soon," Alex said. "Eric's coming later."

"Excuse me?" said Jenny. "Alex, you invited Eric?"

Alex said, "Well, yes. It's okay, isn't it?"

Jenny didn't reply. She didn't like Eric very much.

Faye and David arrived. "Hi, when does the party start?" asked David.

"Well," said Jenny. "It's not really a party. Just a few friends are coming here."

Faye said, "I invited Kerry and Sarah. They're coming later."

"Oh," replied Jenny. She was angry. She thought, "Why did Faye invite them? She didn't ask me! I wanted just a few people. Now lots of people are coming."

"Sorry," said Faye. "They're your friends, so I thought it was okay."

Jenny thought, "Well, I can't tell them not to come now, can I?"

"It's okay," she said. But she wasn't happy.

John and Tyler arrived with their guitars. She was very surprised when she saw the guitars. "Oh, you brought your guitars," she said.
"Yes. We thought we could play some music together," said Tyler.
"Is that okay?" he asked.
"Well, not really," she said. "My parents don't know you're coming here. I don't want anybody to make any noise. Mrs. Smith's coming here soon."
"Oh, I see," said Tyler. "So, you want us to play quietly."
"Well. Yes, I do. Very quietly," Jenny said. She thought, "I don't want them to play at all!"
"Sure, I promise we'll be quiet," said Tyler. "We don't want you to get into trouble."

Jenny, Alex, and Daniela gave some drinks to everybody.
They put out some food. Tyler, David, and John started
playing music. They could play very well.
"Daniela, come and sing with us," said Tyler. "You're a
good singer."
Daniela looked at Jenny. She knew Jenny did not want
people to make any noise. Then Daniela smiled.
Jenny knew her friend wanted to sing. Jenny could not
say no.
"It's okay, Daniela," she said. But she was not pleased.

The party became noisier. Everybody was having a good time. Jenny was having a good time, too.

"It's a little noisy, but it's okay," she thought. "Everybody's having fun." She tried to forget her worries.

Faye said hello to Yoon-Hee and her brother, Ji-Sung, and their friend, Adib. Kerry came, too.

"Oh, no. More people," thought Jenny. But she said, "Hello."

"Thanks for the party," said Yoon-Hee.

"You're welcome," said Jenny. But really she didn't want them to come.

Tyler was taking some things into the kitchen. David did not see him. David hit him, and the drinks and food fell on the floor.

"Oh, no!" said David. "I'm so sorry, Jenny. I'll clean it up."
Jenny was angry with Tyler and David, but she said nothing.
"It was an accident," she thought. "People have accidents. It's okay. I have time to clean it up before my parents come back tomorrow."
"Don't worry," she said. "But please clean it up, okay?"
She thought, "I hope no more people come."

Just then, there was a loud noise outside. Daniela looked out the window.

"It's Gemma and Ryan Walsh, and their friends. They're all coming here!" she said.

"Oh no!" said Jenny. "Who told them to come?"

"Well, Gemma knows about the party," said Daniela. "I guess she thought it was okay to tell her brother, Ryan. So I guess he asked his friends to come, too."

"But *I* didn't invite them, did I?" said Jenny angrily.

Ryan, Gemma, and their friends came in the house. Jenny did not say hello. She was angry, but she said nothing. "What are you doing here?" Daniela asked.

"We came for the party. Thanks, Jenny. Hi, everybody! Sorry we're late!" said Ryan.

Jenny said nothing. She was too angry to speak.

Then she thought, "Why didn't I say anything? I should tell them to leave. I don't want them here. But I don't want them to be angry with me. I want to be their friend. What do I do?"

"Hi, everybody!" said Ryan's friend, Scott. "It's time to party!"

"Yes! Let's party!" said Ryan excitedly. Everybody looked at them.

Ryan put a CD in the CD player. "Let's listen to some dance music," he said.

"Good idea, Ryan," said his friends, Eric and Mike. They pushed the tables and chairs to the wall. They made a place to dance.

"Oh no! Look at all these people!" thought Jenny. "What are they doing to my house?" She saw Eric moving the table.

"Please don't move anything," she said.

"It's okay. I'm only moving it here," said Eric. "It's not heavy. It's not too much trouble, is it?"

Jenny didn't reply.

Some people started dancing. Other people gave out the drinks.
Everybody was having a good time. Everybody, but not Jenny.
She was really angry. She thought, "I don't want these people in
my house. I don't want a party. I hate this. It's all a big mistake.
How can I tell them to go? But they're my school friends, and
they'll be angry if I tell them to go now." Jenny did not know
what to do.

Daniela saw Jenny was not happy. "You're not okay, Jenny, are
you?" asked Daniela.

"Umm . . . I'm okay," she lied.

Daniela knew Jenny was unhappy because so many people were
at her house.

The party got noisier and noisier. The music got louder and louder. People started shouting and dancing. They were not careful with their drinks and food. Ryan's drink fell on the floor, but he didn't say sorry.

Scott asked, "Jenny, why aren't you dancing? You can dance, can't you?"

"Umm . . . I don't want to," she said. She was thinking, "I don't want *anybody* to dance. I just want them to go home. Look at my house! What will my parents say?" She was very worried.

"There's no more food," Eric said. "I'm hungry. What's in the kitchen?"

Eric and Mike went into the kitchen. They took out some food and started eating it.

"Hey! Don't touch that!" said Daniela, coldly. "That's not yours, is it?"

"But I'm hungry," said Mike. "It's okay, it's only food."

"Put that down!" said Daniela. "If you want some food, go and buy it!" Daniela was really angry.

Ryan and Jenny walked into the kitchen. "Where's the food?" Ryan asked.

"No!" said Jenny. "You're not eating my family's food!"

More people were dancing and laughing now. They were making a lot of noise. They were having a good time. The music was very loud.

"What do I do now?" she thought. "I want them to be happy, and I don't want to stop them having fun. But this is *my* house! My parents don't know about the party, so I'm going to be in big trouble when they get back tomorrow."

Just then, Kerry came to Jenny. "Jenny, somebody's at the door. It's a woman," she said.

"Oh, Mrs. Smith," said Jenny. "Tell everybody to be quiet, please."

Kerry told everybody to be quiet. Then Jenny opened the door.
"Oh, hello, Mrs. Smith. How are you?" she asked.
"I'm well, thank you. But what's that noise?" asked Mrs. Smith.
Jenny asked, "Umm . . . what noise?"
"I heard a lot of noise. You're having a party, aren't you?" asked Mrs. Smith.
"Umm . . . no. My friends, Daniela and Alex, are here. We're watching a movie," Jenny lied. "The noise is from the television."
"Oh, I see. Well, please be quiet," said Mrs. Smith.
"I'm sorry, Mrs. Smith," replied Jenny. "Goodbye."

But they weren't quiet. The party was getting noisier than before. Jenny thought, "I want this party to end. This is terrible." She felt terrible, too. Then things got worse.

Eric was not looking and he broke a small vase into pieces.

"Oh, no! That's my Dad's favorite vase!" said Jenny.

"Sorry," said Eric. "But it's not very nice, is it?"

Jenny got angrier. "That's not important," she said. "You broke it, and you'll pay for it!" Jenny nearly cried because she was so angry.

More people started dancing. Then people started taking drinks and food from the kitchen. And more people came. Jenny didn't know what to do. "I only wanted six people, and now there are 20! They won't listen to me. What can I do? I can't ask them to go home, can I?"

Just then Daniela came to her. She was holding the phone. "It's for you!" said Daniela. She gave the phone to Jenny.

Jenny answered the phone. "Hello?" she said. Daniela was telling
everybody to be quiet.

"Oh, Mom. It's you!" Jenny was very surprised. "How are you,
Mom?" she asked. "I'm fine. Daniela's here and we're studying
hard."

Jenny's mother said, "Good. But Jessica's sick. We're coming home.
We'll be back in 30 minutes."

"You're coming home? Tonight?" she said. "Oh! Oh! Umm . . .
okay! See you then! Bye!"

Suddenly, Jenny turned the music off. Everybody looked at her. Her face was dark red with anger. "Look! This is NOT a party!" she said angrily. "This is not fair. I didn't want a party. I just wanted a quiet time with a few friends. I just wanted to watch a movie. And now the house is dirty."

Everybody was shocked. They just listened.

"I told my parents a lie. I said we are watching a movie. I didn't tell them I'm having a party! If they find out I'm having a party, they'll be really angry and I'll be in big trouble!"

She continued, "That was my mother on the phone. My family's coming back in 30 minutes."

"Quick!" said Daniela. "Let's clean the house! Put all the tables and chairs back. Everybody help."

Ryan, Gemma, and their friends said, "We're going now. Thanks for the party, Jenny. See you in class."

"Wait! No, you're not going home. You'll stay here and clean the house. You must help!" said Jenny angrily.

"It's your house, isn't it? You clean it!" said Ryan.

"CLEAN THE HOUSE!" Jenny ordered strongly. "NOW! Do it, or I'll call the police. I didn't invite you!!"

Everybody was shocked. They started to clean the house.

"Ryan and Scott, you clean the kitchen," Jenny said. "Eric, you put back the tables and chairs. The other people can clean the floors and tables. I want the house clean when my parents come home." Nobody said anything. They were scared of Jenny now. Alex cleaned the tables. Eric and Scott put the chairs back in another room.

"Hurry!" said Jenny. "They'll be coming back soon."

"I'll never have a party again," she thought.

Everybody worked hard and fast. Ryan and Scott worked hard in the kitchen. The others picked up the food and drinks.

"We finished!" said Ryan.

"No," said Jenny. "Look, there's more there." She pointed at something to clean.

"Ryan! Wash it, please," she said. "And hurry. My parents will be home soon."

They worked very hard. Soon the house was nearly clean again.

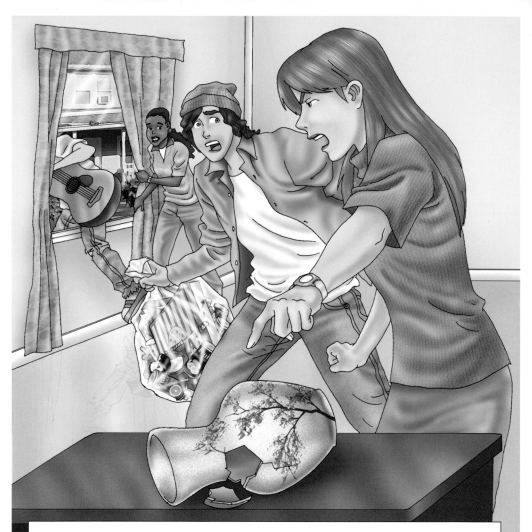

Kerry said, "Jenny, quick! Your parents are here."

Jenny said, "Everybody, quick! Go home. Hurry! And take your things with you."

Everybody went out. Some people went out through the window.

Jenny spoke to Eric. "Eric, don't forget to bring some money for the broken vase tomorrow!"

Eric said, "Umm . . . okay." He ran out of the house.

Alex started the movie and Daniela sat down.

Just then, Jenny's parents came in the door.

"Hi, Jenny. We're back," said her mother. "Is everything okay?" she asked.

"Oh! Hi, Mom, Dad!" she said. "How's Jessica? Is she okay?"

Her father said, "Yes, she's better now."

"Hello, Daniela, Alex," said Mrs. Martin. "Did you enjoy the movie?" she asked.

"Hello. Yes, it was . . . umm . . . great," said Daniela.

"Oh, Dad," Jenny said. "I broke your vase. I'm sorry. I'll pay for it."

Her father replied, "Oh, Jenny. That was my best vase." He was very sad.

Jenny's mother looked around the house. "Everything looks okay," she said.

"Jenny, when I was younger and my parents went away, I always had a secret party," said her mother.

Jenny was surprised. "Oh really, Mom? You had parties?"

"Of course. That's how I met your father," she said. "We met at a secret party when my parents were away."

Jenny said, "Wow, I didn't know that."

"But you didn't have a party, did you?" said her mother.

"Us? Oh no, we just watched the movie, didn't we, Alex?" said Jenny, looking at Alex. Alex looked back.

"That's right," he said.

Her mother smiled.